Discovering
Cultures

Korea

Sarah De Capua

BENCHMARK **B**OOKS

MARSHALL CAVENDISH
NEW YORK

Marshall Cavendish
99 White Plains Road
Tarrytown, New York 10591-9001
www.marshallcavendish.com

Library of Congress Cataloging-in-Publication Data

De Capua, Sarah.
Korea / Sarah De Capua.
p. cm. — (Discovering cultures)
Includes bibliographical references and index.
ISBN 0-7614-1794-X
1. Korea—Juvenile literature. 2. Korea (South)—Juvenile literature. 3. Korea (North)—Juvenile literature. 4. Korea.
I. Title. II. Series.
DS902.D43 2005
951.9—dc22   2004006140

Photo Research by Candlepants Incorporated
Cover Photo: Jose Fuste Raga/*Corbis*

The photographs in this book are used by permission and through the courtesy of; *Corbis*: Bohemian Picturemakers, 1, 26; Chris Lisle, 6, 36, 43 (top left); Setboun, 7, 20, 42 (right), 43 (lower left); Reuters, 9,10, 43 (center), 44; Catherine Karnow, 12 (left), 22, 31; Ludovic Maisant, 13; Janet Wishnetsky, 24; Wolfgang Kaehler, 25, 32, 43 (lower right); Neil Beer, 27; John Van Hasselt, 29, 30 (left); Issei Kato, 30 (right); Lee-Jae-Won/Reuters, 33. *The Image Works*: Bob Daemerich, 4; Baumgarten/Imapress/Vario, 11, 18; Hinata Haga/HAGA, 12 (right); The British Museum/Topham-HIP, 14; Eva & Marcel Malherbe, 15, 17; John Nordell, 16; Topham, 19, 42 (left); Hideo Haga/HAGA, 34, 35, 37. *Craig J. Brown/Index Stock Imagery*: 8. *Sharon Smith/Envision*: 21. *Craig J. Brown*: 38, 45, back cover.

Cover: *Namdaemun Gate, Seoul, South Korea;* Title page: *Two young Korean girls smile for the camera.*

Map and illustrations by Ian Warpole
Book design by Virginia Pope

Printed in China
1 3 5 6 4 2

Turn the Pages...

Where in the World Is Korea?

Korea is located on the continent of Asia. A continent is one of the seven large landmasses on Earth. Korea is a *peninsula* that sticks out 600 miles (966 kilometers) into the sea. It is divided into two countries: North Korea and South Korea. Between North and South Korea is an area called the Demilitarized Zone (DMZ). The DMZ is a narrow strip of land just 2.5 miles (4 km) wide. It stretches across the entire peninsula for 150 miles (241 km). It was created at the end of the Korean War (1950–1953) to separate North Korea and South Korea. The DMZ is fenced with razor wire and is guarded on both sides so that no one crosses without permission.

North Korea is a little smaller than the state of Mississippi. It shares a border with China and Russia in the north. The Sea of Japan is to the east. The DMZ and South Korea lie to the south. The Yellow Sea, which is also called the West Sea, borders North Korea on the west.

The DMZ between North Korea and South Korea

Map of Korea

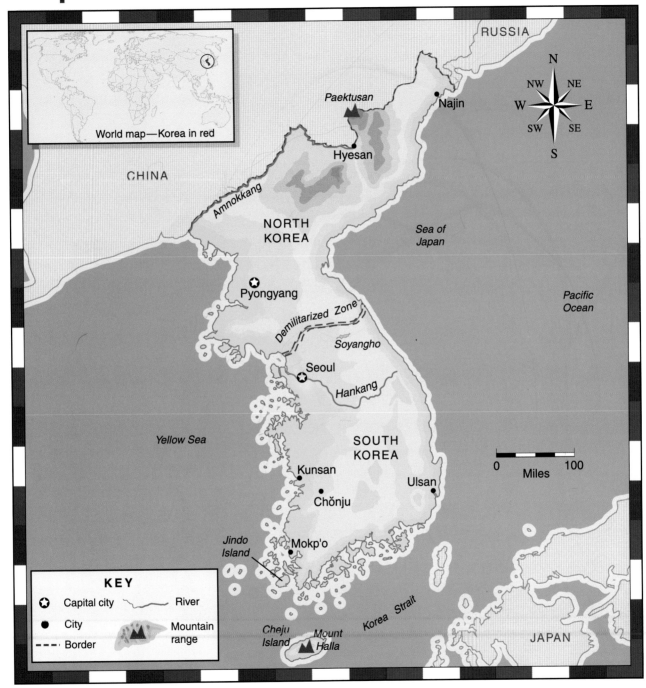

World map—Korea in red

RUSSIA

CHINA

Paektusan ▲▲
Najin

Hyesan

NORTH KOREA

Amnokkang

Sea of Japan

N
NW NE
W E
SW SE
S

⚝ Pyongyang

Demilitarized Zone

Soyangho

Pacific Ocean

⚝ Seoul

Hankang

Yellow Sea

SOUTH KOREA

0   100
Miles

Kunsan

Chŏnju

Ulsan

Jindo Island

Mokp'o

Korea Strait

Cheju Island   *Mount Halla* ▲

JAPAN

KEY
⚝ Capital city   River
● City   Mountain range
--- Border

5

High mountains covered with forests are found in North Korea. Its highest mountain is Paektusan, which rises 9,003 feet (2,744 meters) above sea level. Minerals such as coal are mined in North Korea. Only a little land is good for farming. North Korea has hot summers and long, dry, cold winters. Autumn and spring are short, but colorful, seasons.

South Korea is a little larger than Indiana. South Korea borders the DMZ and North Korea on the north. The Sea of Japan, or East Sea, lies to the east. Like North Korea, the Yellow Sea borders South Korea on the west. Off its coasts are thousands of tiny islands that also belong to South Korea. Farms on the plains in the southwestern part of the country provide most of the people's food. The southern Yellow Sea provides shellfish and edible seaweed to South Korea. To the east and south are waters filled with fish, such as shrimp, salmon, and squid.

Much of South Korea is covered with hills and mountains, but they are not as high as those in North Korea. South Korea's highest mountain is a volcano called Mount Halla. It is on Cheju Island, off the southern coast. Mount Halla is 6,600 feet (1,950 m) tall.

Like North Korea, South Korea has hot summers and long, cold winters. Winter is not as cold

Rock formations in the mountains of South Korea

A village along South Korea's Hankang

in South Korea as it is in North Korea. South Korea's dry air makes the snow disappear, so it does not usually get too deep.

There are many lakes and rivers in Korea. The longest river in North Korea is the Amnokkang. It is 493 miles (803 km) long. Other major rivers include the Yalukang and the Taedongkang. North Korea has many man-made lakes. The largest natural lake is Chonji, at the top of Paektusan.

The Hankang is the longest river in South Korea. It is 321 miles (517 km) long. Other major rivers are the Kŭmkang, Nakdongkang, and Sŏmjinkang. The Soyangho and Ch'ungjuho are major man-made lakes.

Korean plant life changes from place to place, depending on the climate. In the cold mountains, juniper and spruce trees grow tall. In warm places, there are pine and poplar trees. Fruit trees include apple, pear, peach, and orange trees. Gingko trees, whose leaves turn yellow in autumn, also grow nuts. Korea's most famous plant is ginseng. Its roots are believed to increase strength and health. As a result, ginseng is used in many foods, drinks, and medicines. The Rose of Sharon, South Korea's national flower, blooms throughout the summer.

Korea is home to a variety of birds and animals. A type of woodpecker and the Manchurian crane have been named "living national treasures" in South Korea. This means they are protected by the government. Herons are found throughout Korea. Wildcats and brown bears thrive in the DMZ. In the mountains, deer, weasels, badgers, boars, and bears can be found. There are also many kinds of snakes.

Ginseng is one of Korea's most important crops.

The Korean Jindo Dog

The Korean Jindo dog is a wild dog from Jindo Island, off the coast of South Korea. It is also known as the Chindo Gae or Jindo Gae. No one knows how the dogs were first brought to Jindo Island, but they have lived there for hundreds of years.

Jindos are medium-sized dogs. They weigh about 40 pounds (18 kilograms). They may be white, black, yellow, spotted, or black and tan. Their ears stand up on their own when they are between four and six months old. Their coat is medium length, and their tails curl up over their backs.

The Jindo Gae is a smart, loyal dog. It loves its owner and is unhappy if given away. There are many stories of Jindos running away from new owners and finding their way back to their "real" homes. One Jindo Gae in South Korea traveled 200 miles (322 km) over two months to get back to its home! The Jindo Gae's loyalty makes it an excellent watchdog.

What Makes Korea Korean?

Today, about 22 million people live in North Korea. About 48 million people make their home in South Korea. North Koreans call Korea Chosŏn, which means "land of the morning calm." South Koreans call it Hanguk, which means "great nation."

The official language of Korea is Korean. However, there are differences in the language in the two Koreas. North Koreans speak a form of Korean using some different words and grammar than South Koreans. The Korean language includes many Chinese words. However, North Koreans do not use Chinese characters in newspapers and magazines. South Koreans do use Chinese characters in everyday printed materials.

Many non-Koreans live in Korea. The largest group of non-Koreans is the Chinese in South Korea. In recent years, more and more Chinese and South Asians have moved to South Korea looking for work. A large group of people from the American military also lives

A South Korean boy holds a sign written in Korean.

The North Korean flag and a picture of the country's leader hang above this public square in Pyongyang, North Korea's capital.

there. Thousands of U.S. soldiers are stationed in South Korea. They help to patrol the DMZ.

North Korea's official name is the Democratic People's Republic of Korea. Its government is *Communist*. The government is made up of three branches: the executive, the legislative, and the judicial. The head of the executive branch is a *dictator*. He runs the country.

South Korea's official name is the Republic of Korea. Like the United States, its government is a *republic*. Also like the United States, the government is made up of three branches: the executive, the legislative, and the judicial. The head of the executive branch is a president elected by the people. The president is the leader of the country.

The government of North Korea does not allow religion. However, it has allowed some religious groups to make it look like there is religious freedom in the country. A small number of North Koreans follow Buddhist, Christian, or folk religions. Folk religions include the belief that spirits live in nature.

South Koreans have religious freedom. They follow Roman Catholicism, Protestantism, or other branches of Christianity. Some are Buddhists, while a few practice *Confucianism*. Folk religions are also followed. Many South Koreans combine parts of Christianity, Buddhism, and folk religions.

Music, dance, literature, and art are important to Korean culture. Korean folk music is used in celebrations and *rituals*. The two most popular instruments in traditional Korean music are the *kŭmungo* and the *kayagŭm*. Both are

A Buddhist monk

Playing the changgo

Performing a traditional Korean folk dance

flat boxes with strings stretched across. The strings are plucked with a pick or with the fingers. Another well-known Korean instrument is the *changgo*. The changgo is an hourglass drum that can be hung around the neck and struck with drumsticks.

Three kinds of traditional Korean dances are ritual, folk, and court. Ritual dances come from Confucian and Buddhist customs. Folk dances are performed in colorful costumes to celebrate important events, such as harvests. Court dances are slow. Long ago, they were performed for the country's rulers.

Many famous writers have come from Korea. In North Korea, Li Yong Giu writes about North Korean history. Chong-shik Lee writes about North Korean history and government. In South Korea, a famous poet, Sowŏl Kim, wrote about nature. Other writers, such as Kyung-nim Shin and Kyong-ni Park, wrote about the South Korean government and Korean life. The best-known writer of children's stories and songs in North and South Korean was Yoon Suk-joong.

Korean art uses symbols that stand for a long life. These symbols include the sun, the moon, clouds, water, rocks, bamboo, and cranes. They are used in painting, embroidery, and pottery. Perhaps the best-known art form in Korea is celadon pottery, which Koreans have been making since around the year 1050. People all over the world collect celadon pottery.

Most South Koreans wear American-style clothing, including suits, pants, and shirts with colorful neckties for men. Women wear suits, dresses, skirts, and blouses. Jeans and T-shirts are popular when Koreans are not at work. In North Korea, men and women mostly wear American-style clothes.

North Korea sells products such as minerals and military equipment to other countries. South Korea sells electronics, cars, clothing, and fish. South Korea sells more products to the United States than to any other country in the world.

Hanbok

On special occasions, Koreans wear traditional dress called *hanbok*. Hanbok is usually brightly colored, and comes in different styles for men and women. For men, hanbok is usually a short jacket worn with loose-fitting pants that are tied at the ankles. The pants have a belt made of wide cloth. Women wear a short jacket over a long flowing skirt. A child's hanbok is a smaller version of an adult's hanbok.

In South Korea, hanbok is worn on holidays such as Lunar New Year and Chusŏk (Thanksgiving). It is also worn when visiting older relatives, such as grandparents, as a sign of respect. A few older Koreans and some North Korean women wear hanbok every day.

Living in Korea

For much of Korea's history, most of the people lived and worked on the farms of landowners. The most important crop was rice, Korea's main food. Today's North Korean farmers live and work on farms owned by the government. They are not able

Rice paddies in a South Korean coastal village

to grow much food because of a long drought. This period of little rain began in the mid-1990s. South Korean farmers own small pieces of land—usually about 2 acres (.8 hectare) each. Most Koreans, however, have moved from the country-side to work in factories in the cities.

Railroads are the main way people in North Korea get from one city to another. Few North Koreans own cars, so most roads in North Korea are not paved. People within cities and towns walk or ride bicycles to get from place to place. While railroads are used throughout South Korea, cars are common in that country. Paved roads help South Koreans get from one place to another quickly. Because city streets are so crowded with cars, buses, and taxis, many people in the cities walk or ride a bicycle.

A crowded street in Seoul, South Korea

City-dwelling Koreans in both countries live mostly in apartment buildings. Some live in houses outside the big cities. Because so many Koreans live in the cities, their apartments are usually small. A sofa, coffee table, television, and stereo fill the living room, while American-style beds and dressers are found in the bedrooms. Some Koreans sleep on the floor on a mattress called a yo, which is rolled

A North Korean farmer in front of her home

up during the daytime. The floor is a warm place to sleep because homes are heated by pipes under the floor.

Most South Korean homes include a computer. Few North Koreans have computers. This is because the government does not want the people to get information from the outside world through the Internet.

Most Koreans sit in chairs around kitchen tables to eat their meals. In some homes, and in Korean restaurants, the people eat their meals off low tables while they are seated on cushions on the floor. Koreans always take off their shoes before they enter a home or a temple.

In the countryside, Koreans live in villages and small towns. South Koreans grow rice, barley, and vegetables such as cabbage and radishes. North Koreans try

The North Korean capital of Pyongyang

to grow as much food as they can, including rice, vegetables, and fruit. North and South Koreans in coastal villages make their living by fishing.

Family ties are important to North and South Koreans. Many members of the same family often live in the same neighborhood. While fathers work outside the home, mothers usually work at home, caring for the house and children. For 100 days after a baby is born, only family members may see the child. After 100 days, a daylong ceremony is held. At that time, neighbors and friends may visit the baby.

In North Korea, Pyongyang is the capital city and the economic, cultural, and political center of the country. The city has many monuments, statues, museums, and one of the largest stadiums in the world.

The busy city of Seoul looks much like many large cities in North America.

Seoul is the capital city of South Korea and the center of South Korean life. Mixed in with the modern buildings are very old palaces and temples. The Hankang flows through the city. Visitors enjoy modern theme parks, museums, art galleries, and festivals.

A typical Korean meal is made up of rice, vegetables, and fruit. Koreans near the coast add fish to their meals. The national dish of both North and South Korea is kimchi. Kimchi is a spicy dish usually made of pickled cabbage or radishes. It is seasoned with garlic, red peppers, and ginger. Kimchi is no longer common in North Korea because of food shortages caused by the drought. Other countries, including the United States, have tried to help by sending food, but the North Korean government has not given it to the people. Millions of North Koreans have starved to death. Many survive by eating grass, roots, and tree bark. No one knows when the drought and lack of food will end.

Korean foods for sale at an outdoor market

This woman is preparing seaweed for sale.

In South Korea, rice is the main ingredient in meals. Soups are made with vegetable broth and meat, shellfish, or vegetables. *Bulgogi* (barbecued beef) and *kalbi* (barbecued pork ribs) are the most popular meat dishes. Bulgogi and kalbi are made with ginger, garlic, and onions. Small pieces of bulgogi and rice are wrapped in lettuce leaves and eaten by hand. *Banch'an* (side dishes) are eaten with the main meals. These usually include vegetables, meats, seaweed, bean curd, or seafood. Usually seven or eight side dishes are served with every meal.

South Koreans may drink a cup of tea after eating. North Koreans like to drink tea, too, when it is available. Neither North nor South Koreans eat sweets for dessert. Instead, they enjoy fresh fruit. On holidays and special occasions in South Korea, dessert may be made up of small cakes of sweetened rice and nuts.

Let's Eat!
Ttokʼhwachʼae (Rice-Cake Fruit Cups)

Ask an adult to help you prepare this recipe. Always remember to wash your hands with soap and water before you begin.

Ingredients:

1/2 cup rice flour

1/2 teaspoon salt

2 1/2 cups water,
plus additional hot water

1/2 cup sugar

1 knob fresh ginger

raisins

pine nuts

1 medium-sized apple

1 large plum

1 medium-sized peach

In a saucepan, heat 2 1/2 cups water until boiling. While water is heating, knead rice flour, salt, and additional hot water, a little at a time, into a soft dough. Shape the dough into small round balls. Place some raisins and pine nuts onto each piece and reshape into round balls. Use a spoon to carefully place the balls into the boiling water. Boil for 5 to 8 minutes. Remove the balls and rinse them immediately in cold water. Place each ball on a paper-towel-covered plate after rinsing.

Allow the water on the stove to continue boiling. Add the sugar and ginger. Boil until it turns into syrup, stirring occasionally. Remove the saucepan from the heat and let cool. Cut the fruits into bite-sized pieces. Place the rice-cake balls and fruit pieces in a bowl and pour the syrup over them to serve.

School Days

All children in North Korea must go to school for eleven years. They start school at age five. Children attend one year of kindergarten, four years of primary school, and six years of secondary school. Students in primary school, which North Koreans call people's school, study the Korean language, history, mathematics, physical education, art, music, and Communism. After people's school, students enter either a regular secondary school or one that specializes in music, art, or foreign languages. These schools also teach subjects such as history and mathematics. Students in all secondary and specialty schools in North Korea learn English.

Beginning at the age of sixteen, North Korean men must join the country's military for at least seven years. Women have recently been required to join as well. Students who are not able to join the military may continue their education. But they have to receive permission from the government. The government decides what the students will study. For example, a student who

Schoolboys in South Korea

Korean primary school students

received good grades in math and science in secondary school will be sent to medical school or to learn to develop weapons for the North Korean military.

All children in South Korea must go to school until they finish ninth grade. Education is divided into four levels: six years of primary school, three years of middle school, three years of high school, and four years of college. Children can attend preschool until they begin school at age six. Elementary schools are free. South Korean students in elementary school study Korean, English, social studies, math, science, physical education, music, and fine arts. They also receive moral education. This teaches them to be good citizens, to treat others fairly, and to respect the country's laws and traditions.

Fees are charged in the middle and high schools, as well as in college or technical schools. Military service of just over two years is required of all young Korean

Korean students study hard in school.

men. They usually attend college for two years, complete their military service, then finish the final two years of college.

Students in North Korea wear uniforms to school. They go six days a week, Monday through Saturday. In South Korea, most students wear uniforms, whether they attend public, private, or religious school. South Korean students attend classes five days a week, Monday through Friday. The school day begins at about 8:00 A.M. and ends at about 3:00 P.M. In North Korea, Saturday school hours are from about 8:00 A.M. to 12:00 or 1:00 P.M. In both North and South Korea, the school year is divided into two parts. The first half, or semester, starts in March and lasts through June. The second semester begins in September and ends in late December. During July and August, students have summer vacation. From the end of December through February is winter vacation.

In both North and South Korea, students are expected to work hard at school. They do not have many chores at home. When they are not at school, children in both countries play games and sports or do homework. Many South Korean students take private lessons in art, music, or foreign language. Only the wealthiest North Korean students are able to take private lessons.

The Legend of Tangun

Schoolchildren in North and South Korea learn about the famous *legend* of Tangun. It describes how Korea was founded long ago. The legend says that more than four thousand years ago, a bear and a tiger prayed to Hwanin, the divine creator, to make them human. Hwanin's son, Hwanung, heard their prayers and came down to Earth to give them the secret to becoming human.

Hwanung told them that to become human they had to eat garlic and an herb called mugwort and stay out of the sun for 100 days. The bear and the tiger ate the garlic and mugwort and went inside a dark cave. The tiger grew impatient. He left the cave and never became human. The bear stayed in the cave for the full 100 days and turned into a beautiful woman named Ungnyŏ.

Ungnyŏ wanted to have a child. She prayed to Hwanung, who heard her prayers. Hwanung turned himself into a man and married Ungnyŏ. In 2333 B.C., they had a son, and Ungnyŏ named him Tangun.

Tangun became the first human king of Korea. He named his kingdom Chosŏn and made his capital in present-day Pyongyang. Tangun ruled Chosŏn for 1,200 years and taught the people how to farm and care for animals. He also built a huge *altar* on Mount Mani, a mountain on Kanghwa Island. In 1122 B.C., Tangun gave up his rule over Chosŏn and became a mountain god.

Today, visitors who hike to the top of Mount Mani can see the remains of an altar. Although most Koreans believe the story of Tangun is only a legend, the South Korean government protects the altar as an official national treasure.

Just for Fun

Korea has all four seasons: winter, spring, summer, and fall. Winter is usually colder in North Korea than South Korea. Winter sports such as skiing, ice-skating, and speed skating are popular in South Korea. In warm weather, Koreans in both countries enjoy hiking, mountain climbing, and bike riding. South Koreans who live near the coasts swim, water-ski, and windsurf in the ocean. Summer resorts on the west coast of North Korea are popular places for those who live nearby. North Koreans are not allowed to travel within their country without government

Mountain climbing in North Korea

These boys play on a South Korean soccer team.

permission, so most do not go far from home for vacation. There are not a lot of public parks in Korea, because there is not enough land. But many apartment buildings have playgrounds where children can play.

The North Korean government controls all parts of North Korean life. Radio, television, newspapers, and magazines all are owned by the Communist government. The government must approve of everything the people hear, see, and read. Villages have loudspeakers over which Communist radio stations are heard. Anything that goes against Communism is not allowed.

South Korea has much more freedom than North Korea. South Koreans are free to choose their own activities. They spend their time enjoying video games, movies, theater, concerts, dance performances, and sporting events.

Many Korean games were first played in China long ago. Two board games are *changgi* and *paduk*. Changgi is the Korean version of chess. Paduk is played with

Players in a 2003 women's World Cup volleyball match

A young Korean soccer fan

small black-and-white stones. The North Korean government allows the people to play changgi and paduk.

In sports, soccer is the most popular, followed by baseball, volleyball, and table tennis (Ping-Pong). Golf is popular in South Korea. Even though there is not a lot of land, there are many golf courses in that country. Many Koreans in both countries practice tae kwon do—an ancient form of self-defense.

In North Korea, people exercise and play sports at government-owned gyms. The Communist government pays athletes such as boxers, wrestlers, and weight

Shoppers in a department store in Seoul, South Korea

lifters to train and compete for the country. Winning athletes receive cars or large apartments as rewards from the government.

In South Korean cities, people shop in department stores or outdoor market-places. In the marketplaces, they can buy clothing, food, jewelry, and crafts. In Seoul, for example, the streets and sidewalks are always crowded with people working, shopping, or visiting museums. Visitors to Seoul enjoy touring the sites

Tourists visit Kyungbok Palace in Seoul.

of four very old palaces. North Korean cities have a few department stores, but there is little to buy. Outdoor markets are not common in North Korea.

Did you know that karaoke machines came to the United States from Asia? Karaoke started in Japan, but it is popular in South Korea. In some cities and towns, karaoke halls are favorite places to visit. They are open from early in the morning until late at night. Entire families go to them, especially on Sundays, to spend a fun day together.

Tae kwon do

Tae kwon do means "the way of feet and fists." It is one of the most popular martial arts in the world. Tae kwon do began in Korea more than two thousand years ago. Members of the military developed this way to fight that used bare hands and feet instead of weapons. Tae kwon do is not just about fighting, however. Students learn difficult moves and show respect for the people they are competing against. People who study and practice tae kwon do wear uniforms of loose white cotton pants and matching tops. Colored belts, worn with the uniforms, show the wearer's skill level. A white belt means a student is a beginner. Experienced students work to earn many different levels of black belt. Black belts stand for the highest level of skill and ability in tae kwon do.

Let's Celebrate!

In North Korea, there are two national holidays. May Day is celebrated on May 1. Parades showing North Korea's military strength attract thousands to Pyongyang. On September 9, North Koreans celebrate the founding of the Democratic People's Republic of Korea.

Festival performers in masks and hanbok

Korean children in traditional dress enjoying a cultural festival

Some Korean festivals take place in the lunar calendar. The lunar calendar is based on the Moon's trip around Earth. The Moon travels completely around Earth once every twenty-nine to thirty days. So, each month in the lunar calendar is only twenty-nine or thirty days long.

In South Korea, the first big holiday in the year is Lunar New Year in late January or early February. This three-day holiday is called Sŏllal. On Sŏllal, people dress up in hanbok and visit older relatives. Sŏllal celebrations are a time when families gather to eat large meals and play games. Grown-ups give gifts of money to their children and young relatives.

Colorful lanterns hanging outside a temple to honor Buddha's birthday

In North and South Korea, Buddha's Birthday is celebrated on the eighth day of the fourth lunar month, usually May. It honors Buddha, the founder of *Buddhism*. The holiday is often called the Feast of the Lanterns. Many colorful paper lanterns decorate Buddhist temples, as well as homes and streets.

National holidays in South Korea celebrate important events in Korean history. March 1 is Independence Movement Day. This is the day Koreans celebrate their 1919 fight against the Japanese. Japan invaded Korea in 1910 and ruled over it until 1945. Liberation and Independence Day is celebrated on August 15. It marks the day Japanese rule ended. It also marks the day in 1948 when the Republic of Korea was founded.

In South Korea, May 5 is Children's Day. Children have the day off from school and receive gifts from their parents. Chusŏk (Thanksgiving) is celebrated in the lunar month of September. Christmas is celebrated on December 25 in North and South Korea, but it is not a religious holiday in North Korea.

Children play traditional instruments at many South Korean festivals.

Girls dressed in hanbok playing a South Korean game

Tol is a South Korean celebration of a child's first birthday. The child is dressed in hanbok and seated in front of a table. The table is covered with food and objects such as money, books, pens and pencils, thread, and toys. The child is encouraged to reach for something on the table. If the child picks up the money, it is believed he or she will grow up to be rich. If the child chooses a book, he or she will do well in school. Choosing a pen or pencil means the child will become a writer. Thread means he or she will live a long life. The ceremony is a happy time for the child's family and friends. It is followed by a large feast. The guests give gifts to the child and money to the parents.

How Old Would You Be in Korea?

Koreans figure out their ages by saying that a person is in the first year when he or she is born. Therefore, a newborn girl is said to be "one," though it is meant that she is really in her first year of life. She becomes "two" not on her next birthday, but on the next New Year. So, it is possible that a child born in December, being "one," can actually turn "two" in January.

Another way to understand the Korean system is to think of how many years a person has "known." A person born in 2004 has known that year as "one," 2005 as "two," and so on. As a result, when a Korean says his or her age in years, it is one or two years older than it would be in North America.

39

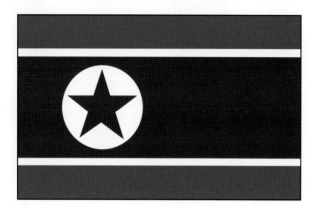

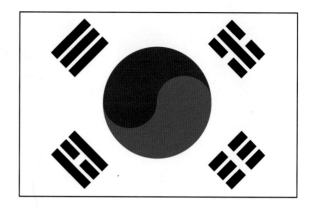

The North Korean flag has three bands—blue at the top, red in the middle, and blue at the bottom. The red band is edged in white. On one side of the red band is a white circle with a red, five-pointed star inside. The red color and red star stand for Communism. The white stands for purity. The blue stands for the wish for peace and friendship.

The South Korean flag is white with a circle in the center. The circle is red on top and blue on the bottom. It stands for balance in the universe. In each corner is a group of black lines, called a trigram. The trigram in the top left corner stands for heaven. The trigram in the bottom right corner stands for earth. The trigram in the upper right corner stands for water. The trigram in the bottom left corner stands for fire. The heaven and earth trigrams, and the fire and water trigrams, balance each other.

The won is North Korea's form of money. The exchange rate changes often, but in 2004, two North Korean won equaled one U.S. dollar. South Korea's money is also called the won, but it is different from North Korea's won. In 2004, 1,162 South Korean won equaled one U.S. dollar.

Count in Korean

English	Korean	Say it like this:
one	hana	hah-nah
two	dul	dool
three	set	set
four	net	net
five	dasŏt	dah-suht
six	yŏsŏt	yuh-suht
seven	ilgop	il-gop
eight	yŏdŏl	yuh-duhl
nine	ahop	ah-hope
ten	yŏl	yuhl

Glossary

altar   A large table used for religious ceremonies.

Buddhism (BOO-diz-uhm)   A religion based on the teachings of Buddha.

Communist (KOM-yuh-nist)   A government that owns all of a country's homes and businesses.

Confucianism (kuhn-FYOO-shuhn-izm)   A set of teachings by a Chinese philosopher.

dictator   Someone who has complete control of a country, often ruling it unfairly.

legend   A story handed down from earlier times.

peninsula   A piece of land that sticks out from a larger landmass and is surrounded by water.

republic   A form of government in which the people elect their leaders.

ritual   Actions that are always performed in the same way as part of a religious ceremony.

trigram (TRY-gram)   A set of three whole or broken lines that are used as symbols.

41

Fast Facts

Korea is a peninsula that sticks out 600 miles (966 km) into the sea. It is divided into two countries: North Korea and South Korea.

North Korea's official name is the Democratic People's Republic of Korea. Its government is Communist. A dictator runs the country.

South Korea's official name is the Republic of Korea. Like the United States, its government is a republic. The president is the leader of the country.

(Map labels: Paektusan, Najin, Hyesan, Amnokkang, NORTH KOREA, Pyongyang, Demilitarized Zone, Soyangho, Seoul, Hankang, SOUTH KOREA, Kunsan, Ulsan, Chŏnju, Jindo Island, Mokp'o, Cheju Island, Mount Halla, Korea Strait)

In North Korea, Pyongyang is the capital city and the economic, cultural, and political center of the country.

Seoul is the capital city of South Korea and the center of South Korean life.

The North Korean flag

The South Korean flag

In South Korea, 46 percent of the people do not follow a religion, 26 percent are Christian, 26 percent are Buddhist, 1 percent is Confucianist, and 1 percent follows other religions.

Korean money is called the won.

North Korea's highest mountain is Paektusan, which rises 9,003 feet (2,744 m) above sea level.

South Korea's highest mountain is a volcano called Mount Halla. Mount Halla is 6,600 feet (1,950 m) tall.

The official language of Korea is Korean.

The longest river in North Korea is the Amnokkang. It is 493 miles (803 km) long.

The Hankang is the longest river in South Korea. It is 321 miles (517 km) long.

As of July 2004, there were 22,697,553 people living in North Korea and 48,598,175 people living in South Korea.

Proud to Be Korean

Se Ri Pak (1977–)

Se Ri Pak was born in the South Korean city of Taejon. She began playing golf in 1991 at the age of fourteen. She won thirty tournaments in Korea before she became a professional golfer in 1996. She competed in Korea for two more years. Se Ri Pak moved to the United States in 1997 to compete in more professional golf tournaments. She quickly became one of the best women golfers in the world. She has won many major tournaments, including the Women's British Open in 2001 and the Ladies Professional Golf Association (LPGA) Championship in 2002. She now lives in Florida.

King Sejong (1397–1450)

King Sejong ruled Korea from 1418–1450. He was highly educated and encouraged knowledge throughout his kingdom. Advances in history, literature, astronomy, and philosophy occurred during his reign. The most important event of King Sejong's rule was the invention of a Korean alphabet. Before this, Chinese characters were used in Korean writing. The alphabet, which is still in use today, is called hangul. It is made up of fourteen consonants and ten vowels. King Sejong did not invent the alphabet. But he ordered a group of scholars to find a way for Koreans to write without using Chinese symbols. During Sejong's rule, other important inventions included a tool to measure rainfall, a clock, musical instruments, and new ways to do mathematics.

Kwan-Sun Yoo (1902–1920)

Born in the village of Ch'onan, Kwan-Sun Yoo was Korea's most famous woman fighter against the Japanese. She attended Ewha Girls' School, one of Korea's first schools for women. As a teenager, she taught Koreans science and geography, as well as how to read. In 1919, she began organizing marches and protests for Korean independence. She bravely spoke out against the Japanese, whose rule was cruel and unjust. Following one of her speeches, she was arrested by the Japanese and sentenced to three years in prison. While in prison she was tortured. She died in 1920. Though Koreans did not become independent until 1945, they remembered the bravery of Kwan-Sun Yoo and it gave them hope.

Find Out More

Books

Cooking the Korean Way by Okwha Chung and Judy Monroe. Lerner Publications, Minneapolis, Minnesota, 2003.

Korea by Valerie Hill. Mason Crest Publishers, Broomall, Pennsylvania, 2003.

The Korean War by Michael Burgan and Karen Price Hossell. Heinemann Library, Des Plaines, Illinois, 2003.

Land of Morning Calm: Korean Culture Then and Now by John Stickler. Shen's Books and Supplies, Fremont, California, 2003.

Web Sites*

http://www.koreaembassyusa.org

Only South Korea has an embassy in the United States. At this site you will find information about the country and its people. You can even listen to South Korea's national anthem.

http://www.babel.uoregon/yamada/guides/korean.html

Here you will find an introduction to the Korean language, which includes a sound player so you can hear how to say words. Includes many useful pages about the Korean language.

Video

My Family from South Korea. VHS, 20 minutes, 2003.

*All Internet sites were available and accurate when sent to press.

Index

Page numbers for illustrations are in **boldface.**

About the Author

Sarah De Capua is the author of many books, including nonfiction, biographies, geography, and historical titles. She enjoys traveling and writing books about the places she has visited. Born and raised in Connecticut, she now lives in Colorado.

Acknowledgments

My thanks to David and Hyun Bishop for their review of the manuscript and answers to my questions, as well as for sharing their large collection of photographs which helped illustrate life in Korea. Their gracious assistance is deeply appreciated. *Kam-sa hamni-da!*